ROGUE ONE
A STAR WARS STORY

"Rebel spaceships, striking from a hidden base, have won their first victory against the evil Galactic Empire. During the battle, Rebel spies managed to steal secret plans to the Empire's ultimate weapon, the DEATH STAR, an armored space station with enough power to destroy an entire planet." —
The opening crawl of *Star Wars*: Episode IV *A New Hope*

How long have you wondered about the story of how the rebels struck out against the Empire and won that crucial first victory against their oppressors? After nearly 40 years, it is time for that story to be told. It's a tale of spectacular adventure, of war and loss, of evil villains whose deeds have tragic consequences for the innocent and the just. But ultimately it's the story of the resilience and bravery of an extraordinary band of heroes, known collectively as Rogue One.

TITAN EDITORIAL
Editor Jonathan Wilkins
Senior Executive Editor Divinia Fleary
Art Editor Andrew Leung
Copy Editor Simon Hugo
Contributing Editor Neil Edwards
Editorial Assistant Tolly Maggs
Production Manager Obi Onuora
Production Supervisors Maria Pearson & Jackie Flook
Production Assistant Peter James

Art Director Oz Browne
Senior Sales Manager Steve Tothill
Subscriptions Executive Ben Alvarez Turner
Direct Sales & Marketing Manager Ricky Claydon
Brand Manager, Marketing Lucy Ripper
Commercial Manager Michelle Fairlamb
U.S. Advertising Manager Jeni Smith
Publishing Manager Darryl Tothill
Publishing Director Chris Teather
Art Director Troy Alders

Operations Director Leigh Baulch
Executive Director Vivian Cheung
Publisher Nick Landau

LUCASFILM EDITORIAL
Senior Editor Frank Parisi
Editor Brett Rector
Image Archives Newell Todd, Gabrielle Levenson, Erik Sanchez, Bryce Pinkos, Tim Mapp

DISTRIBUTION
US Newsstand: Total Publisher Services, Inc John Dziewiatkowski, 630-851-7683
US Distribution: Source Interlink, Curtis Circulation Company
UK Newsstand: Comag, 01895 444 055
US/UK Direct Sales Market: Diamond Comic Distributors

For more info on advertising contact adinfo@titanemail.com

Rogue One: A Star Wars Story The Official Collector's Edition is published by Titan Magazines, a division of Titan Publishing Group Limited, 144 Southwark Street, London SE1 0UP

For sale in the US, Australia, Canada, UK and Eire

Contents © 2016 Lucasfilm Ltd. & TM. All Rights Reserved.

Titan Authorized User. TMN 13428

U.S. edition printed by Quad.

No part of this publication may be reproduced, stored in a retrieval system, or transmitted, in any form or by any means, without the prior written permission of the publisher.

A CIP catalogue record for this title is available from the British Library.

10 9 8 7 6 5 4 3 2 1

CONTENTS

03 / Intro
06 / The Story So Far
14 / Who Are The Rebels?
20 / Profile - Jyn Erso
26 / Profile - Galen Erso
28 / Profile - Lyra Erso
30 / Profile - Mon Mothma
32 / Profile - Cassian Andor
36 / Profile - Chirrut Îmwe
40 / Profile - Baze Malbus
44 / Profile - Saw Gerrera
46 / Profile - Bodhi Rook
50 / Profile - K-2SO
54 / The Rebel Arsenal
60 / Who Are The Imperials?
62 / Profile - Orson Krennic
66 / Profile - Darth Vader
70 / The Troops
78 / Imperial Technology
85 / The Death Star
91 / Concept Art

THE STORY SO FAR...

The journey to *Rogue One*

THE STORY SO FAR...

THE JOURNEY TO ROGUE ONE

1 /

2 /

3 /

The Phantom Menace

The blockade of a politically insignificant world might seem inconsequential, but the Trade Federation's sanctions against Naboo were to prove pivotal for the future of the galaxy. The planet's young queen, Padmé Amidala, escaped the blockade with the help of Qui-Gon Jinn and Obi-Wan Kenobi—two of the galactic peacekeepers known as Jedi. The queen sought out Naboo's senator, Sheev Palpatine, on the planet Coruscant at the heart of the Galactic Republic, but little did she know the politician was not to be trusted.

Palpatine planted the seeds of distrust in Padmé's mind regarding the leader of the Republic, Chancellor Valorum, persuading her to lead a vote of no confidence against him. This led to Palpatine becoming Supreme Chancellor himself—a development that would eventually prove disastrous for the galaxy.

Padmé returned to Naboo, in order to lead the planet's fight against the Trade Federation. Its liberation was achieved with help from the Jedi, the Gungans (a native Naboo species), and Anakin Skywalker, a Force-sensitive former slave boy that Padmé and her Jedi escorts had met on the planet Tatooine.

In the battle for Naboo, Qui-Gon was killed by Darth Maul, and Obi-Wan defeated Maul. Maul was a Sith, one of the opponents of the Jedi who wielded equal skill with the mysterious power known as the Force, albeit harnessing its dark side, rather than the light. After Qui-Gon's body was cremated, two of the Jedi Council, Yoda and Mace Windu, mused that there are always two Sith—a master and an apprentice—meaning that one must remain…

Attack of the Clones

Qui-Gon's dying wish was that Obi-Wan should train young Anakin as a Jedi, as he believed him to be the Chosen One who would restore balance to the Force. His wish granted, it was a decade later when Obi-Wan and his now adult apprentice (or Padawan) crossed paths with Queen Amidala once again.

It was a time of great unrest in the galaxy, as a Separatist movement, the Confederacy of Independent Systems led by the former Jedi Master Count Dooku, had sprung up in opposition to the Galactic Republic. The Republic's Senate debated an act to establish a standing army, which Padmé, now Senator for Naboo, opposed. As a result, she faced several attempts on her life, the last by an assassin who was herself assassinated.

While Obi-Wan set out to find the assassin's killer, Anakin provided protection for Padmé on Naboo, where the pair fell in love. This love had to be kept secret, as such emotional ties contravened Anakin's Jedi training.

Meanwhile, Obi-Wan followed a trail of clues to the planet Kamino—a world that had been excised from all records—where he discovered a vast army of cloned soldiers that had seemingly been commissioned by a long-dead Jedi Master. The clones were all duplicates of a bounty hunter called Jango Fett, whom Obi-Wan met and fought against on Kamino. ▶

1 / Queen Amidala of the Naboo. 2 / The Trade Federation's droid forces on the attack. 3 / Jedi Master Qui-Gon Jinn, a key protagonist in the Battle of Naboo whose death would influence the events that followed.

THE STORY SO FAR...
THE JOURNEY TO ROGUE ONE

Sensing that his mother, Shmi, was in danger back on Tatooine, Anakin persuaded Padmé to accompany him there, disobeying orders. On Tatooine, he discovered that his mother had been abducted by Tusken Raiders. He located and killed these native tribespeople, but was not in time to save his mother. Jedi Master Yoda sensed a great darkness in the Force when Anakin massacred the Tuskens.

At the same time, Obi-Wan pursued Fett to Geonosis, where he overheard a meeting between Count Dooku and other Separatist leaders and learned that not only were they behind the assassination attempts on Padmé, but they were also amassing a droid army. He was then captured by the Separatists, but had time to transmit his findings to the Jedi Council via Anakin and Padmé, who headed to Geonosis to rescue him, along with the droids C-3PO and R2-D2.

Count Dooku tried to persuade Obi-Wan to join him, telling him the Sith Lord Darth Sidious was now in control of the Senate. However, when Anakin and Padmé arrived they were also captured, and all three were sentenced to death in the Geonosis execution arena. In the nick of time, Mace Windu arrived with a Jedi strike force, but its numbers were soon whittled down by the droid army.

Padmé and the Jedi faced certain death, until Yoda arrived with the clone army, which had been put to use in service of the Republic. Dooku tried to escape with the plans for an ultimate weapon, but he was confronted by Anakin and Obi-Wan in lightsaber combat. The Separatist leader soon outmatched his younger opponents and severed Anakin's right arm.

The two Jedi were saved by the arrival of Yoda, who took on Dooku in a fierce duel. However, Yoda was forced to let his opponent escape when Dooku toppled a pillar in the direction of Anakin and Obi-Wan, requiring all Yoda's Force strength to save them.

Dooku fled to Coruscant, where he met with Darth Sidious. With Darth Maul out of the picture, Dooku had become the Sith Lord's new apprentice, going by the title Darth Tyranus, and had formed the Separatist faction purely to aid the cause of the Sith. Now war was breaking out between the Republic and the Separatists, just as Darth Sidious had planned.

As Yoda and Windu pondered Dooku's warning that Darth Sidious was in control of the Senate, Chancellor Palpatine and others watched the launch of a huge clone fleet. Meanwhile, on Naboo, Padmé and Anakin secretly married, in direct contravention of the Jedi Code...

Revenge of the Sith
After three years, the war between the Republic and the Separatists still raged. Battle culminated in Coruscant's atmosphere, and Chancellor Palpatine was captured and taken on board the Separatist forces' flagship, commanded by the cyborg General Grievous.

Obi-Wan and Anakin fought their way onto the flagship and found both Palpatine and Dooku, engaging the latter in combat. Obi-Wan was knocked unconscious, but Anakin soon had Dooku at his mercy. Encouraged by Palpatine, Anakin cut off Dooku's hands and then his head. Trying to

4 / Anakin Skywalker, a slave boy whose Jedi training would have huge repercussions on the galaxy. 5 / Darth Maul, a Sith Lord whose presence alerted the Jedi of the danger to come. 6 / Jedi Obi-Wan Kenobi and Qui-Gon Jinn battle Darth Maul.

THE STORY SO FAR...

THE JOURNEY TO *ROGUE ONE*

7 /

8 /

9 /

10 /

escape with the chancellor, the Jedi were faced with Grievous, who jettisoned all the escape pods before fleeing himself. Anakin had to pilot the huge ship in order to make an emergency landing on Coruscant.

Once they were safe, Padmé told Anakin that she was pregnant—something else they would have to keep to themselves. Meanwhile, Grievous was ordered by Darth Sidious to move the remaining Separatist leaders to the volcanic planet Mustafar. When Grievous mentioned the death of Dooku/Darth Tyranus, Sidious told him that he would soon have a new, more powerful apprentice.

Anakin began to have nightmares about Padmé dying in childbirth, and vowed to prevent it. Later, he met with Palpatine, who had been granted emergency powers, including control of the Jedi High Council. Palpatine told Anakin that he mistrusted the Council, and appointed him as his representative on it. In contrast, the Council itself declined to make Anakin a Jedi Master, much to his anger. When Obi-Wan told Anakin that the Council wanted him to feed them information about Palpatine, he felt torn by his conflicting loyalties.

Anakin joined Palpatine at the opera, where the chancellor told him Grievous was on the planet Utapau, before engaging him in discussion about the power of the dark side. He played on Anakin's anger towards the Council, and his fears for Padmé, suggesting that the Sith, unlike the Jedi, had the power to prevent death.

Anakin reported the location of Grievous to the Council, which decided to send Obi-Wan to Utapau, rather than his headstrong former Padawan, enraging Anakin further. Before he departed, Obi-Wan told Anakin to be patient—he would become a Jedi Master before long.

Anakin met with Palpatine again, who revealed to him that he was Darth Sidious. Anakin thought about killing him, but did not want to risk losing Padmé as a result, so decided to expose him instead.

As Obi-Wan confronted and killed General Grievous on Utapau, Anakin went to the Jedi Temple on Coruscant and told Windu the truth about Palpatine. Windu assembled several other Jedi Masters to go and arrest Sidious, but refused to allow Anakin to join them, fearing that his judgment was impaired. After they left, Sidious used the Force to reach out to Anakin, telling him that any hope of saving Padmé would be lost if he were to die.

The Jedi Masters confronted Sidious at his office, and he quickly dispatched all but Windu, who battled the Sith Lord ferociously. The Jedi eventually bettered the Sith Lord, and prepared to kill him, but Anakin arrived and pleaded with him not to do so. This gave Sidious the chance to prey on Anakin's fears once again, prompting him to cut off Windu's saber arm so that Sidious could kill him. Having chosen his path, Anakin then pledged himself to Sidious as his new apprentice, Darth Vader. Sidious, who was now badly disfigured by his own Force lightning as a result of his battle with Windu, then sent Vader to the Jedi Temple to kill everybody he found there. He did so, flanked by clone troopers, not even sparing the younglings. ▸

7 / Yoda, the wisest of the Jedi. 8 / Jango Fett, the bounty hunter whose clones formed the Grand Army of the Repbublic. 9 / Clone troopers, soldiers who would go on to betray their generals. 10 / Count Dooku, also known as Darth Tyranus.

THE STORY SO FAR...
THE JOURNEY TO ROGUE ONE

At the same time, Sidious issued an order to his army of clone troopers across the galaxy—to kill the Jedi they had until now fought alongside. The clone troopers obeyed Order 66 without question, wiping out scores of Jedi, with Obi-Wan and Yoda among the only survivors. These two were then helped by Senator Bail Organa to warn any other Jedi from returning to Coruscant…

Anakin went to Padmé and told her that the Jedi were traitors, and that he must go to Mustafar to end the war. Once there, he massacred the Separatists, continuing his descent toward becoming a Sith.

Back on Coruscant, Palpatine informed the Senate that the Jedi had plotted to overthrow them, but would now be hunted down. He decreed that the Republic would be reorganized as the Galactic Empire, and he would be its Emperor.

Obi-Wan and Yoda viewed footage of Vader slaughtering the Jedi, and agreed that the Sith must be destroyed. Obi-Wan insisted he confront Palpatine, but Yoda sent Kenobi to face his former apprentice, his "brother" instead.

Obi-Wan went to Padmé to learn of Skywalker's whereabouts; but even after he revealed Anakin's crimes, Padmé still refused. Seeking answers of her own, Padmé left for Mustafar, not realizing Obi-Wan had stowed away on her ship—and had sensed that she was pregnant.

On Mustafar, Padmé was met by Anakin and was shocked by the change in him. When Obi-Wan made his presence known, Anakin believed he had been betrayed and took his anger out on Padmé, using the Force to subdue and knock her unconscious. Obi-Wan urged him to stop, and the two men argued before engaging in a lightsaber duel across the molten landscape.

As battle raged on Mustafar, Yoda challenged Sidious in the empty Senate chamber, but could not contend with the Sith Lord's vicious onslaught, and was forced to flee the chamber—and Coruscant, again with help from Bail Organa. Meanwhile, Obi-Wan and Anakin's battle ended with the Jedi Master triumphant, and his former Padawan left to die, mutilated and horribly disfigured by lava burns.

However, the man who had been Anakin did not die. After Obi-Wan took his lightsaber and left Mustafar with the injured Padmé, Darth Sidious journeyed to the planet having sensed Vader's peril, and removed his badly injured apprentice to his shuttle.

Padmé died shortly after giving birth to twins, whom she named Luke and Leia. Organa chose to adopt Leia, while Obi-Wan took Luke to be raised by Anakin's stepbrother on Tatooine. Vader, meanwhile, lived on in the most painful way imaginable: mechanized by extreme surgery to become a permanently armored embodiment of the Emperor's will, and tortured by the belief that he had killed his wife on Mustafar.

With Padmé dead and the last vestiges of Anakin buried deep within Darth Vader, both Yoda and Obi-Wan went into exile. The droid C-3PO had his memory wiped and Luke and Leia were raised with no knowledge of their father's true identity. The Empire had triumphed, but, in these two children, there was a new hope for the future…

11 / Anakin Skywalker, a powerful but unstable Jedi. 12 / Sheev Palpatine, the Sith Lord Darth Sidious, who finally stepped out of the shadows to oppress the galaxy. 13 / Darth Vader, the Dark Lord of the Sith.

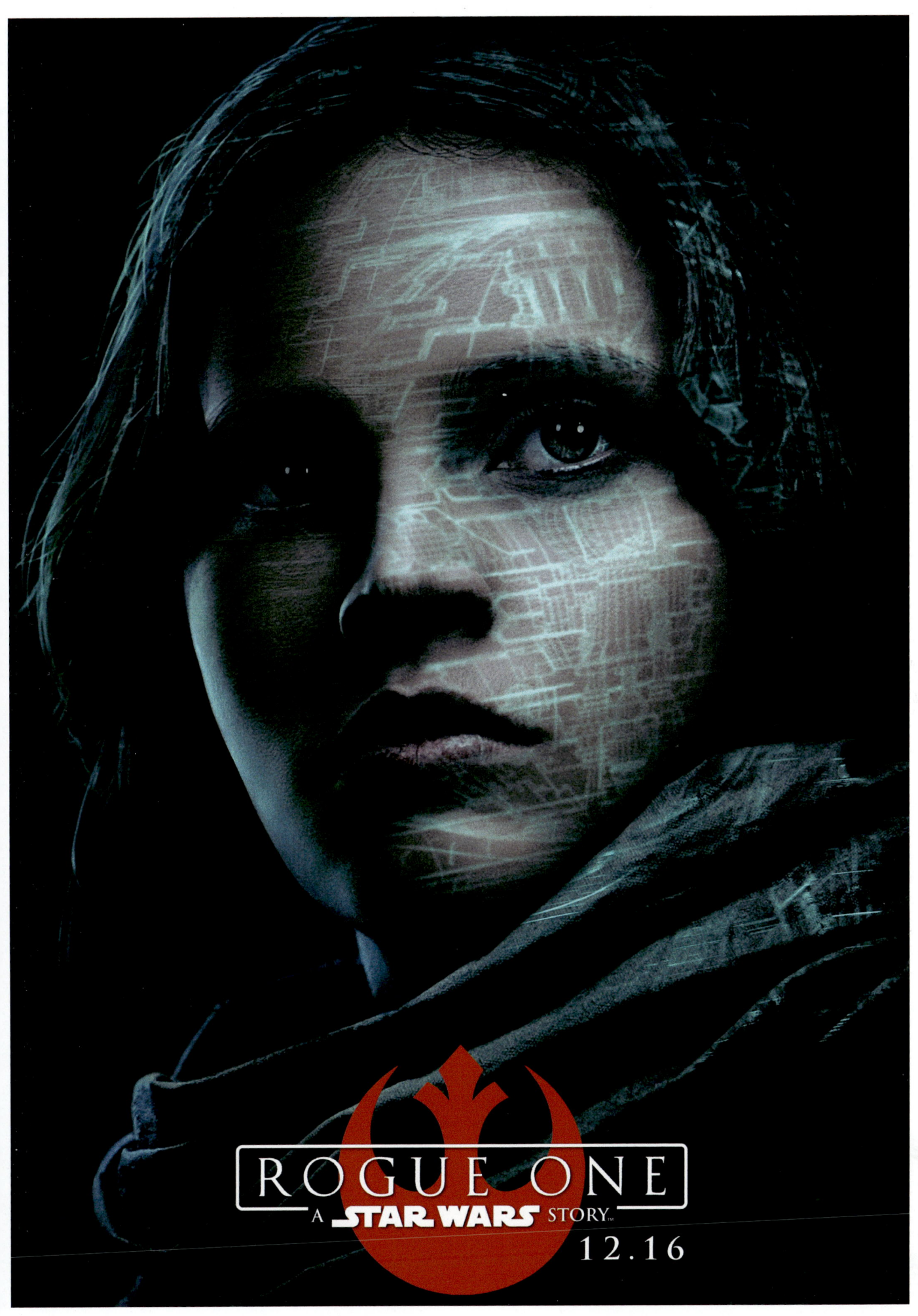

WHO ARE THE REBELS?

They may be the only thing that stands between the Emperor and total galactic domination, but who are the freedom fighters that call themselves the Rebel Alliance?

WHO ARE THE REBELS?
KEY MEMBERS OF THE ALLIANCE

The rebels are a force of opposition against the Galactic Empire, the oppressive regime that grew out of the Galactic Republic. The Empire came about as a result of Sheev Palpatine's maneuverings, first as the Senator of Naboo, then as Supreme Chancellor of the Republic, and finally as Emperor. Unknown to any but his closest advisors, Palpatine was secretly the Sith Lord Darth Sidious, who manipulated galactic events for his own ends.

Once he was elected Supreme Chancellor, Palpatine amassed more and more power for himself, raising a clone army and ordering the execution of the Jedi. But most citizens of the Republic were either fooled by his benevolent public façade or cowed into submission by his more stealthy operations behind the scenes. When Palpatine transformed the Republic into the Galactic Empire and declared himself Emperor, there was no further need for pretense, and any opposition to his rule was ruthlessly extinguished.

However, there were some brave and insightful souls who had worked against Palpatine during his rise to ultimate power. ▶

1 / General Dodonna takes command.

2 / X-wing pilot Zal Dinnes.

3 / Lieutenant Sefla leads his troops against the Empire.

4 / General Draven at a rebel briefing.

5 / X-wing pilots at ease.

16 | ROGUE ONE: A STAR WARS STORY

WHO ARE THE REBELS?
KEY MEMBERS OF THE ALLIANCE

1/
2/
3/
4/

WHO ARE THE REBELS?
KEY MEMBERS OF THE ALLIANCE

► Chief among them were Bail Organa, an Alderaanian senator with a strong sense of justice, and the serene yet steely senator from Chandrila, Mon Mothma.

Mothma had been an outspoken opponent of the Clone Wars against the Confederacy of Independent Systems, and fiercely resisted the granting of emergency powers to Palpatine by the Senate. As the Clone Wars neared their conclusion, Organa, Mothma, and several allies including Senator Padmé Amidala of Naboo met in secret to discuss Palpatine's latest executive orders, which included taking control of the Jedi Council and appointing his own governors to oversee the galaxy's star systems. Though Amidala cautioned the others not to openly oppose Palpatine, it was at this meeting that the seeds for a rebellion against his despotic rule were sown.

By the end of the Clone Wars, the Jedi were almost entirely wiped out, Amidala was dead, and the Republic was reorganized as the Galactic Empire. The worst fears of Mothma and Organa had been realized, and they began to prepare a more active resistance to the Emperor and his forces.

Independent rebel cells began to spring up across the galaxy, and before long most of these joined forces under the leadership of Mothma and Organa, becoming the Alliance to Restore the Republic—otherwise known as the Rebel Alliance.

Mon Mothma and Bail Organa were forced to take their opposition to Palpatine's oppressive regime underground. By this time, Organa's adopted daughter Leia (actually the daughter of Anakin Skywalker) had succeeded her father as the senator for Alderaan, and she also became involved in the Alliance as one of its most important operatives.

Despite her own pacifist leanings, Mon Mothma realized that the Rebellion would need the strength and resources to fight the Empire on its own terms, and under her leadership it began to assemble its own starfleet and other military forces.

When word reached the rebel leader that an Imperial superweapon was in development and near to completion, she saw a chance for the Alliance to strike back against its oppressors and rob them of a final, total victory. For the rebellion, the risks involved would be high, but not to act would be to risk the future of the entire galaxy…

1 / Zal Dinnes (Red Eight).

2 / Heff Tobber (Blue Eight).

3 / Admiral Raddus.

4 / General Davits Draven.

5 / Barion Ranner (Blue Four).

6 / General Jan Dodonna.

JYN ERSO

"THIS IS OUR CHANCE TO MAKE A REAL DIFFERENCE."

JYN ERSO
REBEL WITH A CAUSE?

A rogue and a rebel who might just become a hero, Jyn Erso is enlisted to take part in a seemingly impossible mission.

Jyn Erso was born to Galen and Lyra Erso on the planet Vallt during the Clone Wars, one of the most tumultuous periods in galactic history. Jyn Erso's turbulent start in life offered a taste of what was to come.

Trapped behind enemy lines on Vallt and held captive by Separatist forces, young Jyn and her parents were liberated by Galen's old friend, Orson Krennic, who enlisted Galen to work on a mysterious top secret Imperial project on Coruscant. However, Krennic's kindness was a deception; in reality he was harvesting Galen's genius to create a devastating super-weapon, that the Empire planned to use to hold insurgent forces in line with almost unimaginable brutality. When Galen learned the true nature of the project he was working on, he took Lyra and Jyn and fled the Imperial capital, aided by rebel firebrand, Saw Gerrera.

The family established a new life in hiding on the rural Outer Rim world Lah'mu, eking out a humble existence among fewer

> "May the Force be with us."

than 500 settlers who populated the planet. Despite the world providing an effective hiding place for those looking to avoid the watchful gaze of the Imperial machine, the Erso family were eventually tracked down by Krennic and his squad of Imperial death troopers. Lyra, Jyn's moral compass as she was growing up, was killed, and Galen was taken into captivity, but Jyn managed to escape before being taken off-world by Gerrera, who spirited her away and raised her to be a soldier.

Between the ages of eight and sixteen Erso became a fighter with Saw's militia, as well as a smuggler and petty criminal, adopting a variety of aliases over the years, including Tanith Ponta, Liana Hallik, and Kestrel Dawn. Her training and experience led to her becoming proficient in hand-to-hand combat as well as skilled at improvising with whatever weaponary came to hand, though she favored dual truncheons as her weapons of choice.

After the group suffered a crippling defeat, she was ▶

JYN ERSO

"THIS IS OUR CHANCE TO MAKE A REAL DIFFERENCE."

1/

abandoned by Gerrera. The sudden trauma of losing her mentor left Erso unable to trust others and, not for the first time in her life, she was left alone and isolated.

On her own and without the sense of direction that Saw Gerrera was able to provide, she was captured on Corulag, arrested under the alias Liana Hallick and sentenced to a labor camp on Wobani. It was only the intervention of the rebel Specforce team, commanded by Sergeant Ruescott Melshi, that led to her liberation. Little did she know she was about to be plunged into greater danger than she bargained for.

Enlisted by rebel leaders Mon Mothma and General Davits Draven, she becomes involved in a daring mission to steal the data tapes that hold the schematics of the Empire's Death Star, the exacting and horrific planet-destroying weapon that Jyn's father helped create. With the vital information contained on those tapes, the rebels just might turn the tide of the Imperial's march to galactic dominance... or die trying.

1 / Sergeant Jyn Erso and Captain Cassian Andor pose as pilgrims in the Holy City of Jedha.

2 / Jyn Erso sneaking into position on Eadu.

3 / Jyn Erso in the heat of battle.

4 / Preparing for combat against the forces of Director Krennic.

5 / Rescued by the Rebel Alliance, Jyn embarks on a deadly mission.

JYN ERSO

"THIS IS OUR CHANCE TO MAKE A REAL DIFFERENCE."

2 /

3 /

4 /

5 /

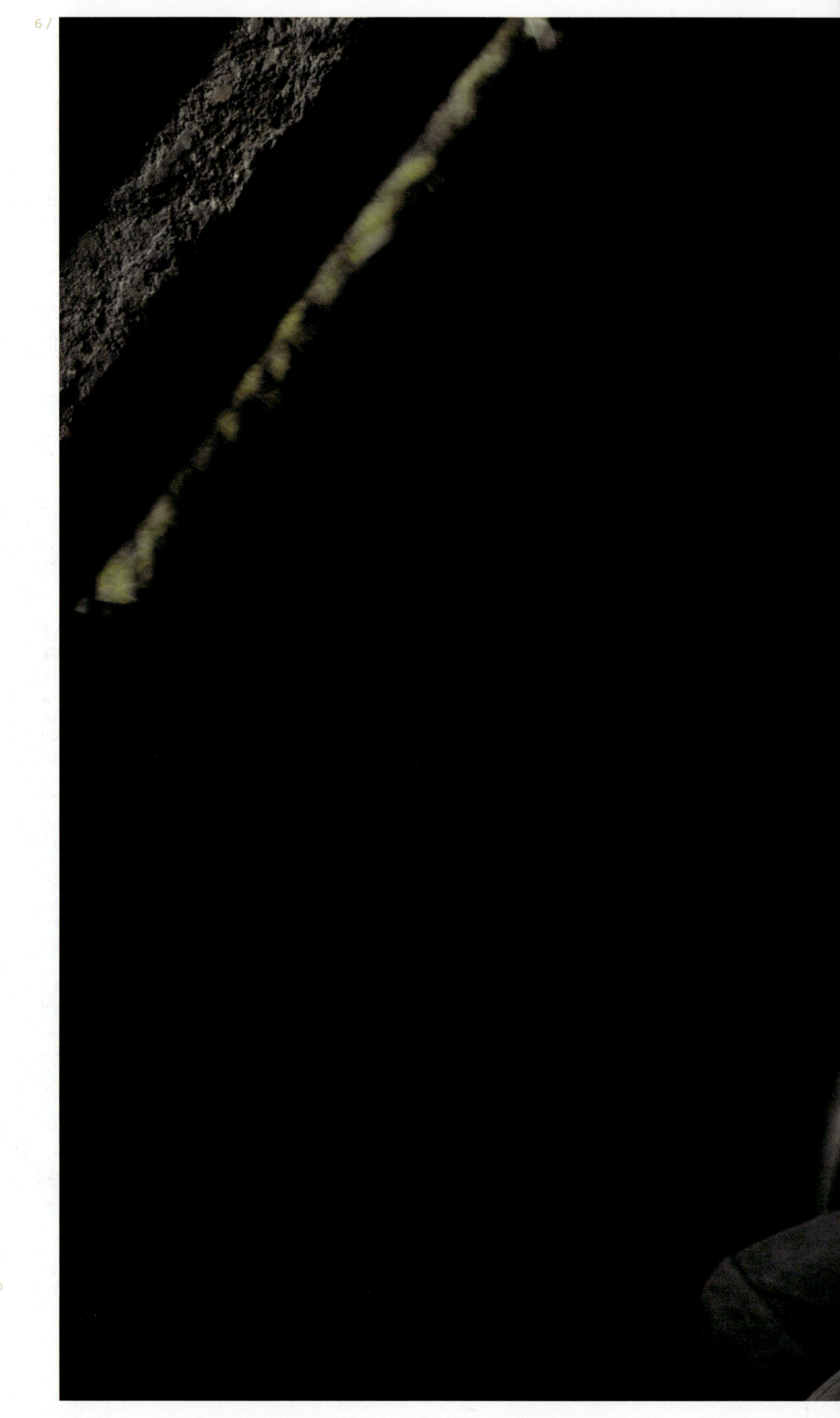

6 / Captured by the Empire, Jyn will soon be rescued and enlisted to help the rebels fight against oppression.

GALEN ERSO

"WE CALL IT THE DEATH STAR… THERE IS NO BETTER NAME."

GALEN ERSO
UNWILLING COLLABORATOR

One of the galaxy's most brilliant minds, Galen Erso is the reluctant genius behind Project Celestial Power, otherwise known as the Death Star.

A genius polymath, Galen Erso has dedicated his life to seeking an unlimited energy supply in an attempt to solve the problem of galactic want and inequality.

At the age of 16 he entered the Futures Program on Brentaal, where he met and befriended a younger student, Orson Krennic. Later, Krennic was instrumental in Galen gaining a visiting professorship at the Institute of Applied Science on Coruscant, where Galen concentrated on research into kyber crystals.

Galen met his future wife Lyra on a field trip to Espinar in search of kyber crystals. During the Clone Wars, the couple and their young daughter, Jyn, were caught behind enemy lines and held captive on the Separatist planet Vallt. They were liberated by Orson Krennic, little realizing that Krennic had in fact manipulated events in order to make Galen indebted to him.

The family returned to their lives on Coruscant while Galen worked for Krennic, but in time, Galen learned the true nature of Project Celestial Power and its connection to the Death Star. He took Lyra and Jyn to the Outer Rim planet Lah'mu. When, after a few years, Krennic tracked him down, Galen refused to return to work on the Death Star. As a result, Lyra was killed, Jyn was taken away by rebel maverick Saw Gerrera, and Galen was forced into effective servitude, heading up a team of scientists on Eadu, researching ways of fusing kyber crystals together and weaponizing them. Years later, he sent a coded transmission, warning the Rebel Alliance that the Death Star's might was ready to be tested…

> " Jyn, whatever I do, I do it to protect you. Do you understand? "

26 | ROGUE ONE: A STAR WARS STORY

LYRA ERSO
"TRUST THE FORCE."

LYRA ERSO
DEFYING THE EMPIRE

A brilliant scientist in her own right, Lyra Erso was also a wife and mother. Wary of the increasing dominance of the Empire across the galaxy, she will do whatever it takes to keep her family safe.

Even before she, Galen, and their daughter Jyn fled Coruscant for the Outer Rim world of Lah'mu, Lyra Erso had become deeply suspicious of the Empire.

Born on Aria Prime, her geological studies at the University of Rudrig not only gave her the opportunity to explore distant worlds, but afforded her a glimpse of the sometimes-ruthless nature of galactic governance. On the planet Espinar she met Galen, acting as guide to his kyber crystal survey team. The pair fell in love and married a year later, settling on Coruscant, where Galen continued his research into energy transformation.

Following the birth of their daughter, the turmoil of the Clone Wars, and the establishment of the Empire, Lyra came to understand that she and Galen were effectively prisoners of the Empire. When Galen realized the horrific true nature of his endeavors on Coruscant, Lyra was more than willing to establish a new life with her family on Lah'mu.

But it was not to be, as Imperial death toopers, led by Director Orson Krennic, eventually tracked the Erso family down, enlisting Galen to assist in the creation of the Empire's weapon.

Ultimately, she sacrificed her own life for Jyn's, dying at the hands of Orson Krennic in order that her daughter might survive.

MON MOTHMA

"WE HAVE A MISSION FOR YOU."

MON MOTHMA
THE SENATOR

A highly principled leader, Mon Mothma's ideals saw her flee from the political landscape into the world of rebellion against the Empire.

The daughter of an arbiter-general in the Galactic Republic and a governor on Chandrila, it is no surprise that Mon Mothma pursued a political career. She became a member of the Galactic Senate at an early age, becoming one of the youngest senators in the chamber.

Fundamentally a loyalist, Mothma began to question what had happened to the state as the Clone Wars brought discord to the galaxy. With Supreme Chancellor Palpatine granted emergency powers, she and others, including Bail Organa, and Padmé Amidala, began meeting in private to decide how best to counter the excesses of Palpatine's rule. It was at these meetings that the seeds of the Rebellion were formed.

There reached a point where Mon Mothma could keep her secrecy no longer, publically accusing the now-Emperor Palpatine of being a "lying executioner."

> "We need to stop this weapon before it is finished."

This blatant, open act of defiance was the breaking point. Already secretly helped to supply the expanding Rebelllion with aid, while carefully avoiding spies who would report their actions to the Imperial Security Bureau Mon Mothma resigned from theSenate, and fled from Coruscant. With good reason, as her words had elevated her to the top of the Imperials' "Most Wanted" list. It was this action that marked the formal beginning of the Rebel Alliance.

Both a political leader and commander-in-chief of the Rebel Alliance forces, Mon Mothma is the head of the Alliance Civil Government, with the title Chief of State. However, as a political leader, she prefers to be known as a senator.

As Emperor Palpatine's exacting and tyrannical rule continued,and the galaxy increasingly suffered, Mon Mothma recieved word of an awesome weapon that, if not stopped, could spell the end of the fledgling Alliance.

CASSIAN ANDOR

"IF YOU'RE REALLY DOING THIS, I WANT TO HELP."

CASSIAN ANDOR
THE REBEL CAPTAIN

A rebel spy whose missions have left their mark on his psyche, Captain Cassian Andor's extensive combat experience is crucial to the mission to steal the Death Star plans.

Born on the planet Fest, Cassian Jeron Andor grew up in the Outer Rim, joining the fight against the Republic after his father was killed at the Carida military academy while protesting against Republic militarism.

He became a member of an insurrectionist cell, running low-level sabotage against Republic forces, which taught him that even the most powerful machinery could be brought down. Years later, he was recruited into the Rebel Alliance by General Draven.

Since then, Andor has largely worked for Alliance Intelligence, undertaking many dangerous missions, from infiltration and reconnaissance to assassination and sabotage. He is also a proven fighter on the battlefield, able to work solo as required, and has established a network of contacts on Imperial worlds.

Often placed in direct contact with the Empire—where the odds of survival are said to be four-

> "It's the trooper that you don't see that will get you."

to-one against—Andor has used many aliases, including Willix, Aach, Joreth Sward, and Fulcrum. His favored weapon is a BlasTech A280 CFE (Covert Field Edition), an adaptable firearm that can be used as a sniper rifle and an assault weapon. He also carries a compact security key hidden in his boot. Always active, he avoids downtime to prevent him from thinking about the nature of some of his more extreme assignments, which include assassinations.

It was through his network of contacts that Andor heard rumors about the Empire concealing shipments of kyber crystals in civilian convoys, which arrived on Kafrene from the Unknown Regions before being dispatched elsewhere. On Kafrene, he tracked down an intelligence source, Tivik, who told him that Bodhi Rook, an Imperial cargo pilot, had defected the day before on Jedha, prompted by an individual named Galen ▶

CASSIAN ANDOR

"IF YOU'RE REALLY DOING THIS, I WANT TO HELP."

Erso. Erso had told Rook to find resistance leader Saw Gerrera and warn him about an impending Imperial weapons test using kyber crystals—an experiment that, if successful, would be powerful enough to destroy an entire planet. Before he could learn any more, Andor and Tivik were interrupted by stormtroopers. Andor killed them—and Tivik—to stop him being taken into Imperial custody. He then returned to Base One on Yavin 4 with his information...

1 /

2 /

1 / Cassian Andor at the rebel base on Yavin 4.

2 / Captain Cassian Andor.

3 / Jyn and Cassian lead the newly formed Rogue One team into battle.

4 / Jyn and Cassian in the Massassi Temple.

5 / A man haunted by his past. Andor takes a moment to reflect on his part in the Rebellion.

34 | ROGUE ONE: A STAR WARS STORY

CASSIAN ANDOR

"IF YOU'RE REALLY DOING THIS, I WANT TO HELP."

CHIRRUT ÎMWE

"I FEAR NOTHING. ALL IS AS THE FORCE WILLS IT."

CHIRRUT ÎMWE
THE TRUE BELIEVER

A spiritual warrior who follows the teachings of the Force, Chirrut Îmwe and his comrade-in-arms, Baze Malbus, fight the oppressive Imperial presence on Jedha.

He may be blind, but Chirrut Îmwe is an expert warrior, able to sense combatants and strike at them with great accuracy, whether it's with his kyber-capped uneti wood staff, his lightbow, or merely his hands and feet. Îmwe is a master of zama-shiwo, otherwise known as "the inward eye of the outward hand," a form of martial arts native to Jedha. Its practice involves the perfection of physical awareness—the ability to control breathing, heart rate and circulation to superhuman levels

The cause of his blindess is something that Îmwe keeps a close secret. In place of his sight, Îmwe relies on both his mental discipline, which allows him to ignore unnecessary information, and a strong physical sense of control that helps him move with

> " The Force is with me and I am with the Force. "

ease through his surroundings.

Îmwe is a member of a near extinct order, the Guardians of the Whills, who are sworn to protect the Temple of the Kyber in the Holy City of Jedha. Despite a powerful sense of loyalty to the Force and a deep-seated respect for the Jedi, Îmwe is wise enough to know that no one could ever claim to truly understand the intricate nature of the Force.

Îmwe wears a Jedha pendent of reforged gold that depicts an ancient symbol of a starbird—a symbol that also represents the Alliance to Restore the Republic.

With his trusty modified bowcaster—a handcrafted lightbow—this warrior monk proves to be a crucial member of the Rogue One team as he joins the fight against the Empire on Scarif.

CHIRRUT ÎMWE

"I FEAR NOTHING. ALL IS AS THE FORCE WILLS IT."

1 /

2 /

CHIRRUT ÎMWE

"I FEAR NOTHING. ALL IS AS THE FORCE WILLS IT."

1 / Baze Malbus and Chirrut Îmwe on Scarif.

2 / Chirrut and the rest of Rogue One going behind enemy lines.

3 / Meeting Jyn Erso.

4 / Two masters of combat... and their assailants.

5 / Face-off against a squadron of stormtroopers.

BAZE MALBUS

"I FIGHT THE EMPIRE NOW."

BAZE MALBUS
THE EX-GUARDIAN

A gruff warrior with a penchant for heavy weaponry, Baze Malbus is a man who has the Empire in his sights.

Once a Guardian of the Whills but now a specialist with energy weapons, Baze Malbus has been transformed from devoted adherent of the Guardians' order to a battle-hardened veteran of numerous hit-and-run attacks on the Imperial forces on Jedha.

Exchanging his religious robes for combat armor, Baze has discarded his faith in favor of a heavy repeating blaster. Despite their obvious differences, his firm friendship with Chirrut Îmwe remains intact. As dedicated to the destruction of the Empire as he is, Baze has little time for either Saw Gerrera's militia or the Rebel Alliance. Instead he focuses his anger—not to mention his blaster—toward the Empire.

Baze's repeating cannons offer the equivalent of five laser rifles' worth of firepower. An illegal weapon for civilians, Baze's cannons are just another

> "They destroyed our home. I will kill them."

symbol of his insurgency and defiance of the Empire. Unlike his friend, Chirrut Îmwe, Baze Malbus has discarded his vestments of the Guardians of the Whills, instead wearing a flight suit and combat armor supplied by a visitor from offworld. In fact, Baze and Chirrut are the perfect partnership, with the "muscle" of Baze's extensive firepower working with Chirrut's more thoughtful, studied approach to combat.

Despite the grim predicament of living under Imperial occupation, Baze maintains a sense of gallows humor and exasperation at his best friend's positive mantras.

Whether blasting at AT-ACTs or stealthily taking down troops on Scarif, Baze Malbus is the kind of warrior that you want, and almost certainly need, to have firmly on your side. You certainly wouldn't want him as an enemy…

BAZE MALBUS

"I FIGHT THE EMPIRE NOW."

1 / With his friend, the spiritual warrior, Chirrut Îmwe.

2 / Showing off some superior firepower!

3 / Baze Malbus takes aim.

4 / Taking action on the war-torn streets of Jedha.

BAZE MALBUS

"I FIGHT THE EMPIRE NOW."

SAW GERRERA

"I'M NOT A TERRORIST. I'M A PATRIOT. AND RESISTANCE IS NOT TERRORISM."

SAW GERRERA
THE REBEL VETERAN

A freedom fighter who is prepared to fight for victory at any cost, Saw Gerrera is a hardened warrior who inspires great loyalty among his comrades.

Leader of the militia on the planet Jedha, Saw Gerrera has waged war on the Empire since its beginnings. Accused by some of being a terrorist, and by others of being a madman, he was trained and equipped by the Jedi Knights to fight the Separatists on his homeworld of Onderon, leading the rebellion there with his sister, Steela.

Already a battle-hardened warrior, Gerrera became utterly merciless following his sister's death and his own torture at the hands of the Separatists. When the Republic became the Empire after the Clone Wars, Onderon was annexed, prompting Saw to lead a new rebellion against his former allies.

For years Gerrera fixated on

> " Save the dream! Save the rebellion! "

clues and rumors about an Imperial superweapon, at one stage getting so close to the truth that the Empire moved the unfinished Death Star from its position above Geonosis. This obsession, together with his questionable actions and methods as a rebel leader, have put Gerrera at odds with the Rebel Alliance, but his militia on Jedha remains fiercely loyal.

Driven by his passion to drive back the Empire, the veteran soldier now relies on a life-support suit to keep him in the fight. Operating from the Catacombs of Cadera, a deserted base in a remote part of Jedha, he commands a unit of warriors united by his powerful leadership.

SAW'S ARMY

WEETEEF CYU-BEE
A sharpshooter specializing in explosives, this Talpini warrior is one of the most destructive rebels in Saw's band.

MOROFF
A mercenary who packs a powerful Vulk TAU-6-23 "Blastmill" rotary blaster canon.

KULLBEE SPEARADO
A mysterious gunslinger, who was recruited on Serralonis and seems to have a shady past...

EUWOOD GOR
Hailing from the planet Alderaan, Euwood Gor was a Rebel Alliance Pathfinder who joined Gerrera on Onderon.

CYCYED OCK
Armed with a vibrorang weapon, Ock has a cybernetic implant that gives him enhanced vision.

LEEVAN TENZA
A Sabat who was part of General Dodonna's rebel force before joining Gerrera, Tenza is a defiant and laconic figure.

BEEZER FORTUNA
The most politically-minded of his clan, this Twi'lek serves as chief strategist to Gerrera's motley unit.

MAGVA YARRO
Magva serves as an expert forward spotter for Saw Gerrera's Cavern Angels squadron.

BODHI ROOK

"IT'S UM ROGUE, ROGUE ONE."

BODHI ROOK
THE DEFECTOR

A defector from the Empire, Bodhi Rook's conscience led him to turn on his former comrades and become a crucial part of the Rebellion.

As an Imperial cargo pilot, Bodhi Rook had an insider's view of the nefarious workings of the Empire. A native of Jedha, he spent two years in flight training at the Terrabe Sector Service Academy, but did not score highly enough to graduate to starfighter academy.

Instead, he stayed at Service Academy for another two years, after which he was granted the rank of ensign and rated ready for cargo transports and shuttles. This was how Rook came to be transporting kyber crystals from Jedha to a top secret Imperial research facility on Eadu, and ferrying cargo between Eadu and another Imperial installation on the planet Scarif.

To distract himself from the evils of the Empire and its pernicious and oppressive influence on his homeworld,

> *"He said I could get right with myself... If I was brave enough."*

Bodhi took up gambling, laying credits on odupiendo races on Jedha. Eventually, his conscience got the better of him, and—encouraged by Galen Erso, who told him about the existence of the Death Star—he defected, surrendering to Saw Gerrera's militia. For his troubles, Rook was subjected to a draining interrogation at the hands of the distrustful Gerrera, before surrendering evidence in the form of a holographic recording.

Practical but nervous, Rook is seen to be not the most eager rebel, but has even less love for the Empire. His in-depth knowledge of the Imperial machine is crucial to the Rebellion, and even his past as a gambler has its uses. Drawn into the mission to seize the plans for the Death Star, it is Rook who comes up with the call sign "Rogue One".

BODHI ROOK

"IT'S UM ROGUE, ROGUE ONE."

BODHI ROOK

"IT'S UM ROGUE, ROGUE ONE."

2 /

3 /

4 /

1 / Bodhi Rook in action on Scarif.

2 / The former Imperial pilot wears an Imperial cog on his sleeve to remind himself of his past.

3 / A reluctant rebel, Rook has even less love for the Empire.

4 / Rook becomes a key member of the Rogue One team.

K-2SO

"YOU ARE BEING RESCUED. PLEASE DO NOT RESIST."

K-2SO
AN IMPERIAL ALLY

A droid who should be an enemy of the rebels, K-2SO is actually one of its most important assets: a reprogrammed spy on the side of the Alliance.

Personally reprogrammed by Captain Cassian Andor, K-2SO is an Imperial combat droid who now fights alongside the Alliance to restore the Rebublic. He is perhaps the only KX-series droid to have been successfully reprogrammed.

Originally created, like all the KX series, by Arakyd Industries, K-2SO was ostensibly designed as a security droid. However, the KX droids' programming secretly included exceptions to the standard in-built droid rules about not harming flesh-and-blood creatures, as well as commandsto defer to Imperial officers, with the result that they were deployed on the battlefield against the rebels. Although programmed to interact

droids are not as well-versed as protocol droids at the intricacies of human-cyborg relations.

Cassian was able to strip out the majority of the Arakyd programming, with the unintended consequence that

> "There is a 97.6 percent chance of failure."

K-2SO is now often brutally honest in his assessments. Humanoid in appearance—albeit in exagerated preportions—the 12-year-old droid K-2SO was

with the ability to operate a range of machinery and equipment. This, in combination with programming that allows him to pilot multiple Imperial vessels, and his innate speed and strength, has made him an invaluable resource on many missions with Cassian Andor.

Although he is a crucial tool in the battle against his former Imperial commanders, he isn't quite trusted enough to be allowed to brandish a blaster.

Despite the fear of combat droids following the Clone Wars, K-2SO is the ideal spy, blending in Imperial territory while reporting back to his rebel masters. A key member of the rebel strike team sent to retrieve the Death Star datatapes, K-2SO

"YOU ARE BEING RESCUED"

K-2SO

"YOU ARE BEING RESCUED. PLEASE DO NOT RESIST."

1 / Captain Cassian Andor, Jyn Erso, and K-2SO.

2 / Cassian Andor, Jyn Erso, and K-2SO infiltrate the Imperial base on Scarif.

3 / K-2SO on Jedha.

4 / The Imperial droid confers with Jyn Erso.

5 / Cassian Andor and the droid he reprogrammed.

K-2SO

"YOU ARE BEING RESCUED. PLEASE DO NOT RESIST."

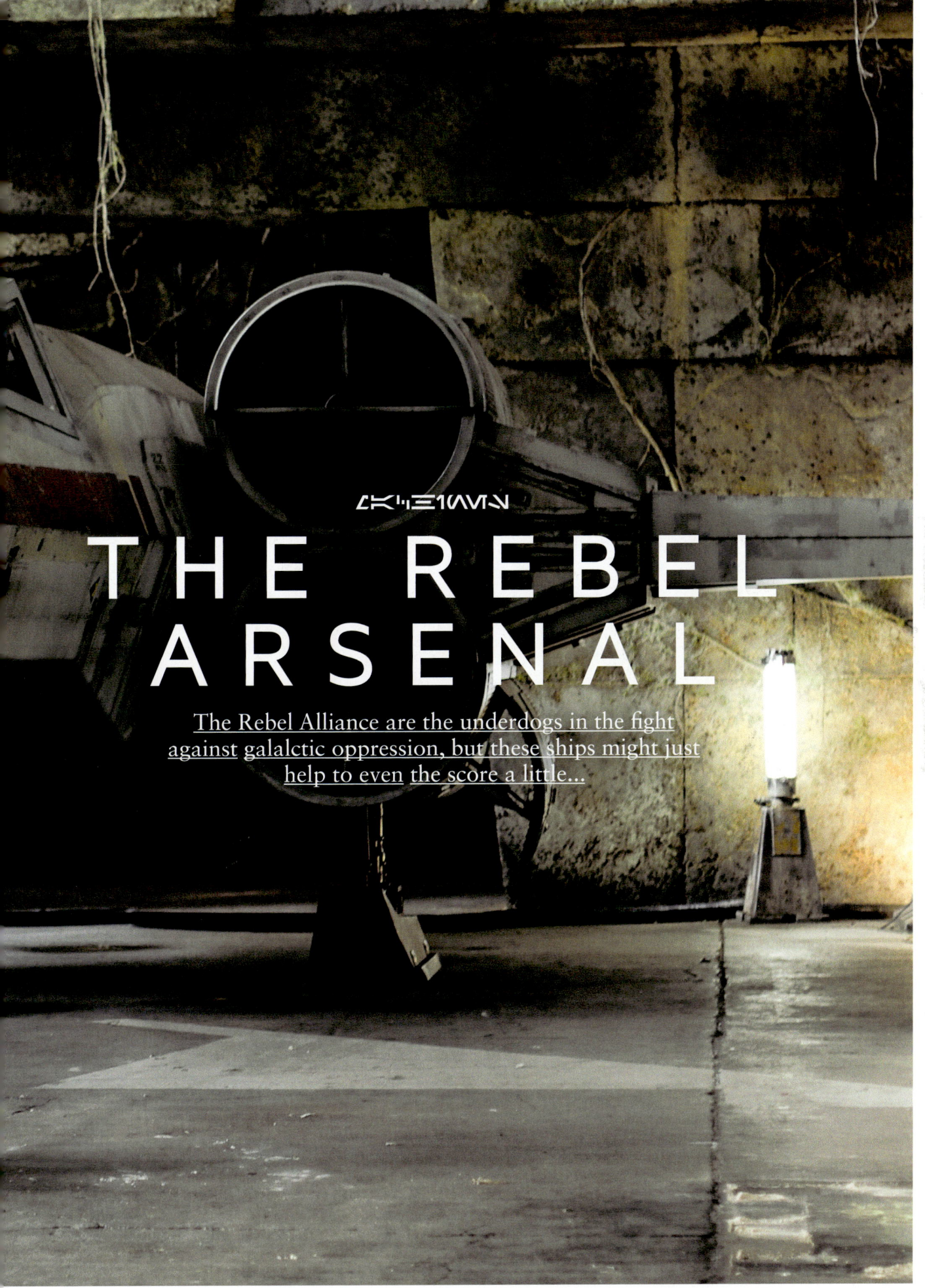

THE REBEL ARSENAL

The Rebel Alliance are the underdogs in the fight against galalctic oppression, but these ships might just help to even the score a little...

THE REBEL ARSENAL

SHIPS OF THE ALLIANCE

T-65 X-WING

The most well-known starfighter in the rebel fleet, Incom's X-wing is perhaps the ultimate ship of its kind: Not only is it fast, maneuverable, well-armed and well-shielded, it is capable of hyperspace flight.

56 | ROGUE ONE: A STAR WARS STORY

BTL Y-WING

Dating back to the Clone Wars, the Y-wing serves as an assault fighter and bomber. The model used by the Alliance to restore the Republic, stripped off the original hull plating and engine nacelles of the earlier models for ease of maintenance.

U-WING

A troop transport and gunship, the U-wing starfighter is a swing-wing vessel capable of penetrating heavy fire zones, to deploy soldiers onto battlefields before providing crucial air support. Well-shielded, the U-wing is not as nimble as a regular starfighter.

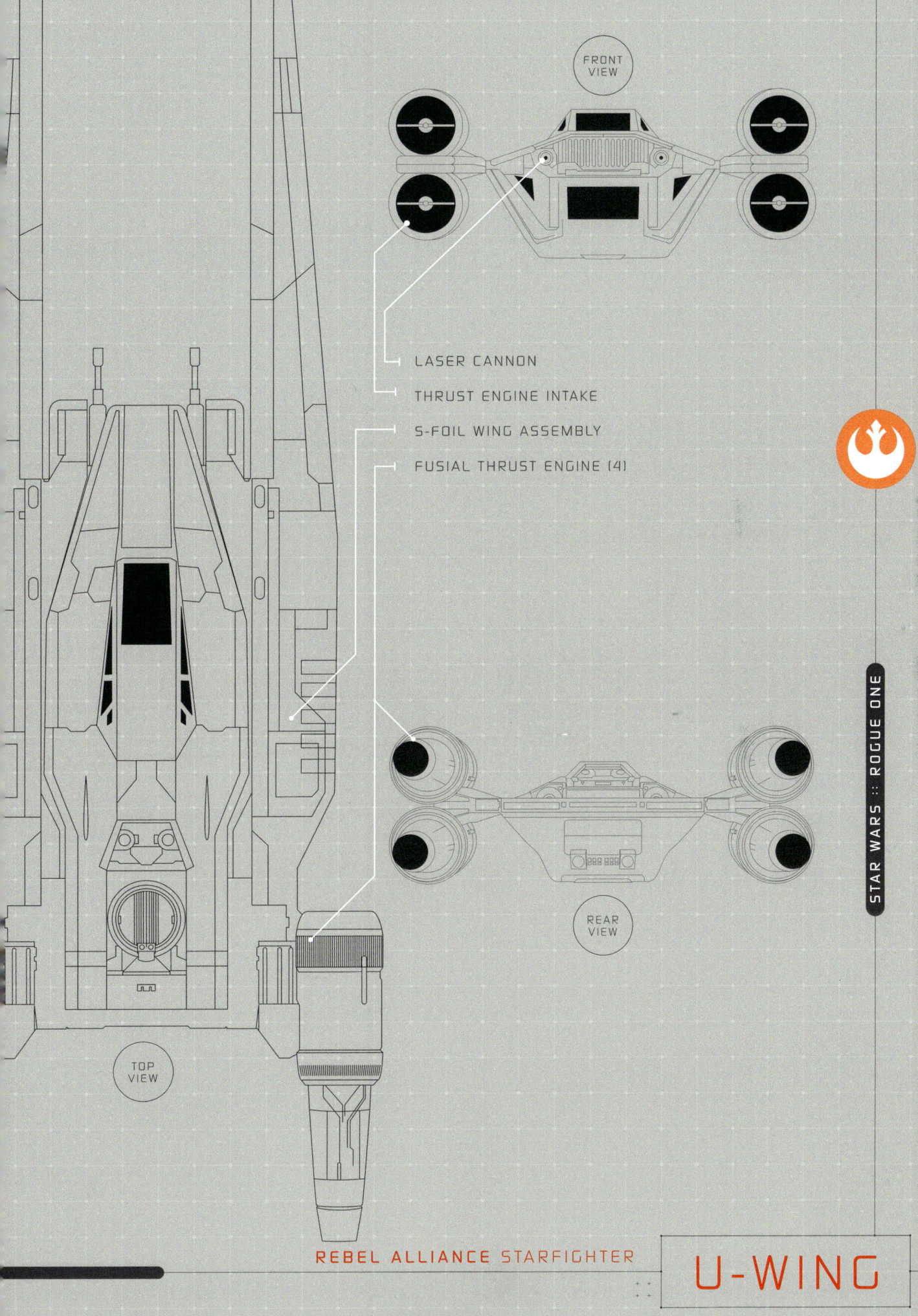

WHO ARE THE IMPERIALS?

For most galactic citizens, the Empire is a faceless sea of stormtroopers, policing their every move. But behind the muscle is a single malevolent mastermind…

WHO ARE THE IMPERIALS?

THE EMPIRE

1 / Stormtroopers and shoretroopers on Scarif.

2 / Death troopers take positions against the enemy.

3 / An Imperial gunner prepares to fire.

4 / Imperial combat tanks patrolling Jedha.

The Empire was once the Galactic Republic, but where the Republic was a democracy, with member planets represented by their own senators, the Empire is a tyrannical regime, ruled over by Emperor Palpatine, who is really the Sith Lord Darth Sidious.

Palpatine gained power by manipulating galactic events, first orchestrating the Invasion of Naboo, then playing the Republic and the Confederacy of Independent Systems against each other to spark the Clone Wars. Once he'd used the Clone Wars to raise an army and suppress opposition to his rule, Palpatine set himself up as Emperor and reshaped the Republic in his own image.

Instead of a Senate, the Emperor now appointed his own ruling council to oversee the day-to-day running of the Empire, as well as assigning planetary governors, sector governors (known as Moffs), and oversector governors (known as Grand Moffs). His Sith apprentice, Darth Vader, held a more diverse brief, acting as the Emperor's enforcer.

Throughout the galaxy, the most obvious symbols of Imperial rule were the stormtroopers, whose great numbers and highly visible, armored presence kept many downtrodden planets in line. Stormtroopers were generally garrisoned on occupied worlds, or served as a mobile force on board Star Destroyers—vast starships that could crush any thoughts of resistance simply by appearing in orbit. While the forerunners of this immense army, the clone troopers, had been explicitly created to serve as soldiers, stormtroopers and other Imperial personnel—such as TIE fighter pilots—were volunteers or draftees.

The Empire soon became known for its hardline approach, enforcing the most minor laws with draconian methods. With harsh customs laws fueling demand for hard-to-find goods, devil-may-care pirates and smugglers flourished at the periphery of the Empire, while more lawful citizens were badly oppressed for lesser infractions.

While some people welcomed the Empire as an antidote to the chaos of the Clone Wars, others recognized it for what it was—an oppressive regime ruled by a power-hungry despot. And though few would openly speak the truth, small cells of resistance slowly began to grow in confidence and numbers, banding together to bravely confront the Empire with the possibility of all-out rebellion…

ORSON KRENNIC

"THE POWER WE ARE DEALING WITH HERE IS IMMEASURABLE."

ORSON KRENNIC
THE DIRECTOR

Ambitious and driven, Orson Krennic's career, reputation, and maybe even his life depend on the completion of the Empire's much-delayed superweapon, the Death Star.

Born in the Sativran City on the planet Lexrul, Orson Callan Krennic is an Imperial officer determined to deliver the ultimate weapon to Emperor Palpatine and win the respect and admiration of his equally ambitious peers.

Highly intelligent but very cruel, Krennic has spent years driven by the desire to realize the Death Star—a project begun decades ago by the Separatists (under the direction of Senator Palpatine) before being adopted by the Empire. To that end, he has assembled a team of unwilling but coerced scientists on Eadu (led by his former friend Galen Erso), and set them the task of harnessing the awesome power of kyber crystals.

Krennic's road to the upper echelons of the Empire began when he studied architecture in the Futures program on the planet Brentaal. It was there that he first met Galen Erso, and where his gift for manipulating others became evident. He went on to work in the design regiment of the Corps

> " We're on the verge of greatness. "

of Engineers, before supervising construction of government headquarters and military facilities on Coruscant during the Clone Wars. Upon joining the Republic's Strategic Advisory Cell as part of the Special Weapons Group, he began to research and test weapons for the Grand Army of the Republic and the Republic Navy. When the Republic became the Empire, Krennic became Director of the Empire's Advanced Weapons Research division.

An outsider among the high-born Imperials of Coruscant society, Krennic is not given to rhetoric and debate, and his highly volatile temper often gets the better of him. This causes great concern among his fellow officers and superiors such as Grand Moff Tarkin. Armed with a non-regulation DT-29 heavy blaster pistol with a custom-fitted macroscope, the Director is not a man to be crossed, and the cold steel of his designs for the Empire very much reflect the man himself.

ORSON KRENNIC

"THE POWER WE ARE DEALING WITH HERE IS IMMEASURABLE."

1 / Director Orson Krennic.

2 / Imperial officers gather to witness the might of the Empire's superweapon.

3 / Director Krennic in a pensive mood.

4 / A moment of contemplation as Orson Krennic considers his destiny.

ORSON KRENNIC

"THE POWER WE ARE DEALING WITH HERE IS IMMEASURABLE."

DARTH VADER

"THE ABILITY TO DESTROY A PLANET IS INSIGNIFICANT NEXT TO THE POWER OF THE FORCE"

DARTH VADER
THE DARK LORD

The Empire's most sinister agent has proved himself to be a loyal servant of Darth Sidious after his defeat on Mustafar.

As the Empire gained strength around the galaxy, Darth Vader proved himself as a feared enforcer. From the ashes of Mustafar rose a warrior even more ruthless and cunning than before, and clad in black imposing armor. The former Jedi commanded his own squadron of stormtroopers, otherwise known as "Vader's Fist," who inspired fear wherever they went.

Five years into the Emperor's iron rule, Vader accompanied his master, Darth Sidious, on a mission to crush the rebellion on Ryloth, led by Cham Syndulla.

Faced with an extreme attack from Twi'lek insurgents, the Sith Lords were forced to crash-land on the forest planet. They were soon attacked by a lylek horde, retreating into a tunnel that was, in fact, the creatures' nest. They stood their ground against a hundred or so lyleks and their queen, killing them before encountering a young Twi'lek girl, Drua. Vader prevented the Emperor killing her, intending to have her guide them to her village, where they were finally able to summon help. Despite being surrounded by Syndulla's forces, relief finally arrived as the Imperials set about quelling the insurgency.

At the Emperor's command, Vader killed the rebels, bringing the Sith Lord's mission on Ryloth to a violent end.

Some time later, The Emperor commanded Vader and Moff Tarkin to investigate an attack on Sentinal Base, an Imperial stronghold in the outer rim. During a misadventure on Murkhana, *Carrion Spike*, Tarkin's personal modified stealth corvette was stolen by dissidents, who Tarkin were sure to be connected to the attack, as well as being supported by a senior member of the Imperial military.

Tarkin and Vader managed to unravel the mystery and Vader executed the culprit, while Tarkin commanded the Star Destroyer *Executrix* as it decimated the dissident fleet.

This led to a newfound mutual respect between the Dark Lord Tarkin and the ambitious officer who was rewarded for his efforts by being promoted to Grand Moff. He was assigned to take command of the construction of the Death Star over Geonosis.

The Hunt

As the Death Star's construction continued, The Emperor sought out the "children of the Force." He commanded Darth Vader to order ▶

DARTH VADER

"THE ABILITY TO DESTROY A PLANET IS INSIGNIFICANT NEXT TO THE POWER OF THE FORCE"

a Grand Inquisitor to hunt down these children and either enlist them into the service of the Empire, or kill them. The Inquisitor promised Vader that his mission would be accomplished.

However, after his mission failed, the Inquisitor killed himself rather than facing Vader's wrath.

Several rebel cells that had united to fight the Empire were revealed when they rescued a small gang of Lothal rebels from an Imperial fleet. As rumors of these events became known, uprisings begun to occur on several worlds, including Lothal.

The Emperor sent Vader to Lothal with Tarkin to end the growing rebellion. Vader concocted a cunning trap which would help him track the Lothal rebels back to their base. The Dark Lord met with Imperial agents Kallus and Minister Maketh Tua, informing Tua that Tarkin would hold her accountable if she failed to stop the rebels.

Gripped by terror, Tua contacted the Lothal rebels, offering them information if they would smuggle her off the planet before she met with Tarkin. The rebels agreed, and returned to Lothal. However, this played directly into Vader's hands as he had intended for the minister to contact the rebels and lure them back to Lothal. He had a bomb placed on Tua's shuttle. Once the rebels arrived, they attempted to escape the planet, only for the bomb to go off as Tua boarded the ship, killing her.

Vader then broadcast the misinformation that the rebels had assassinated Tua. He had Kallus lockdown the planet's spaceport, telling everyone that any ship attempting to escape would be destroyed. Vader knew that the rebels would need to steal a ship in order to escape. He used a shuttle capable of hyperspace travel as bait. When the rebels tried to commandeer it, Vader

1 /

2 /

was ready, confronting them with a small squad of stormtroopers. Vader dueled with the rebel leader, a Jedi named Kanan Jarrus, and his apprentice Ezra Bridger.

Vader easily bested his two opponents. Realizing that they could not win, they stalled Vader long enough to make their escape aboard the shuttle.

Shortly after, the rebels used the shuttle to rendezvous with the rebel fleet. But Vader had been tracking them, and launched an attack on the rebel fleet in his TIE Advanced x1 fighter. The rebels fought back but were no match for the Sith Lord as he disabled the rebel command ship, *Phoenix Home*.

1 / Lord Vader makes his imposing presence felt!

2 / Showing respect to Lord Vader.

3 / The Dark Lord of the Sith: a fearsome figure who inspires terror and obedience in the Imperial navy.

The Lothal rebels boarded their ship, the *Ghost*, and fought back against the Dark Lord in a futile attempt to defeat him. With all seemingly lost, Vader's former apprentice, Ahsoka Tano, combined her powers with Kanan's, using the Force to probe Vader's mind.

As the two former allies became aware of each other, Ahsoka passed out and Vader broke off his attack, instead centering his attention on the *Ghost*. As Vader closed in, his intended prey jumped to hyperspace.

Vader informed Sidious that he had "broken" the rebels, but also revealed to Sidious that Ahsoka Tano was alive. Sidious

DARTH VADER

"THE ABILITY TO DESTROY A PLANET IS INSIGNIFICANT NEXT TO THE POWER OF THE FORCE"

declared that she could lead them to other Jedi who survived the purge of Order 66.

Sidious instructed Vader to send another Inquisitor to hunt the rebels. After several unsuccessful attempts to capture the rebel Jedi, the Fifth Brother and Seventh Sister Inquisitors pursued Jarrus, Bridger and Tano to a Jedi Temple on Lothal. The Inquisitors warned Vader that the Jedi were increasing in their ability to use the Force, but he replied that it would be their undoing.

A Final Battle

Vader sent the two Inquisitors, along with a third, The Eighth Brother, to hunt down Darth Maul, who was located on Malachor, where he had been studying its Sith temple for years. The Zabrak killed the Inquisitors, leading to Vader personally choosing to retrieve the holocron and take possession of the superweapon that was also being sought by Ezra Bridger.

Vader confronted Bridger, quickly disarming him before being interrupted by Tano.

She assured Vader that there were no more Jedi left. As Vader taunted her, stating that Anakin had been weak, Tano responded by battling the Dark Lord, eventually managing to slice through Vader's mask, revealing his partially exposed face and confirming that the he was, indeed, Ahsoka's former master and friend.

As the Temple locked down, Tano said that she would stay with him causing Vader to pause briefly.

The two resumed their fight, as Kanan Jarrus and Ezra Bridger took flight from the chamber as it closed around the two combatants. As they fought, a massive energy discharge consumed the area. Although Tano's fate remains unknown, Darth Vader managed to escape from the Temple...

With the Death Star project under the watchful eye of Emperor Palpatine, Vader is tasked to oversee the officers behind its construction.

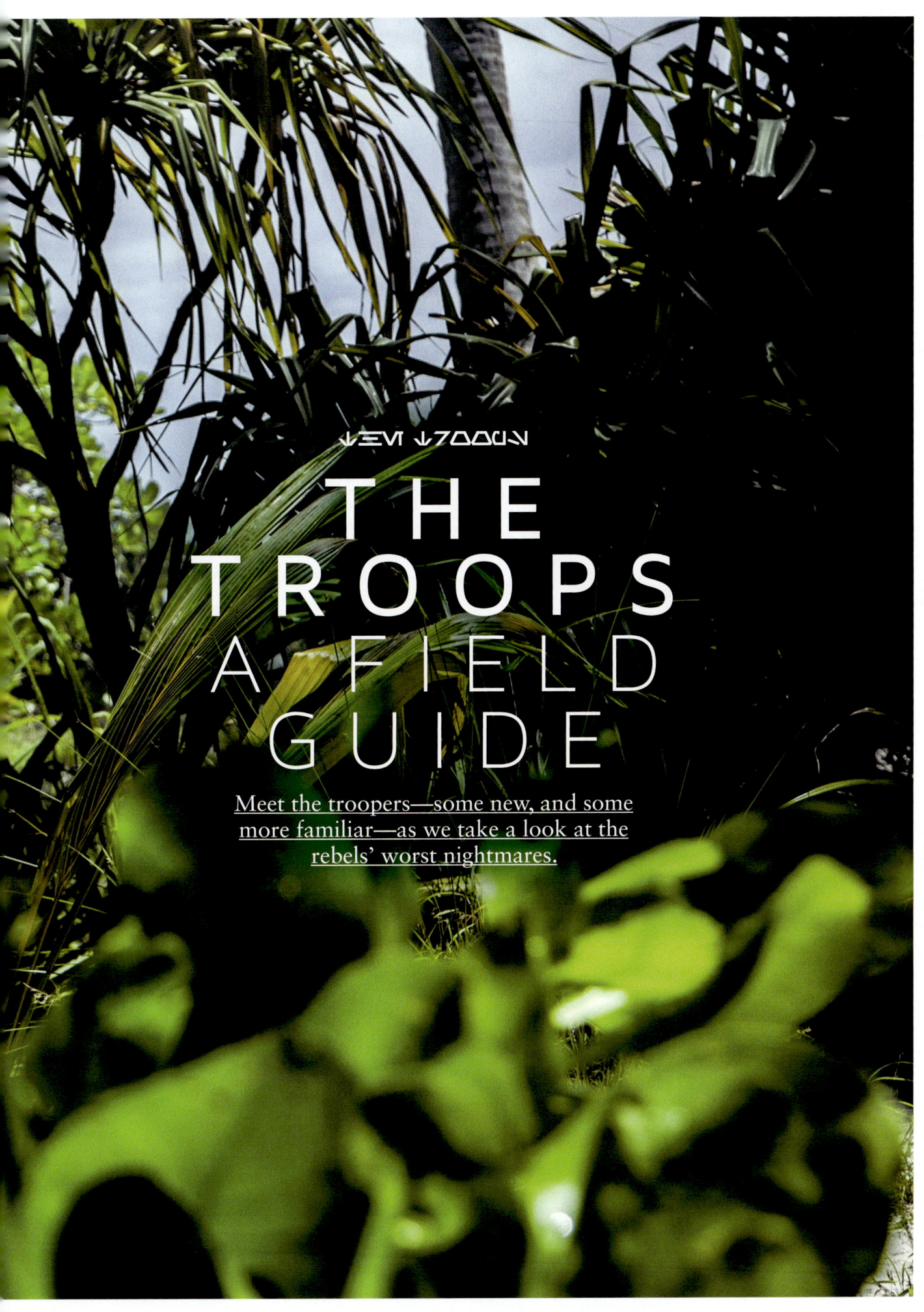

THE TROOPS
A FIELD GUIDE

Meet the troopers—some new, and some more familiar—as we take a look at the rebels' worst nightmares.

STORMTROOPER

The most well-known and easily identifiable of the Empire's elite soldiers, Imperial stormtroopers are the cold enforcers of the Emperor's dark will.

Brandishing powerful blasters, these servants of the Empire are as merciless as they are loyal.

SHORETROOPER

Patroling the luxurious world of Scarif, the shoretroopers are specialist elite stormtroopers. Owing to the highly specific nature of the postings, they are a rare sight in the galaxy. They operate at an effective sergeant rank, which means they are able to command stormtrooper squads.

DEATH TROOPER

Imperial death troopers are specially chosen to protect vital operations and operatives.

Wearing armor formed from plastoid coated in reflec, these troopers are very hard to detect, making them effective when on stealth missions.

IMPERIAL COMBAT DRIVER

Trained to pilot the Empire's ground assault vehicles (GAVs), these combat pilots are lightly armored, relying on their heavily armored vehicles to bear the brunt of any attack.

TIE FIGHTER PILOT

Elite warriors of the skies, TIE fighter pilots undergo rigorous training in order to earn their place in the Imperial navy.

IMPERIAL ROYAL GUARD

Elite soldiers assigned to protect the Emperor, the Imperial Royal Guards are highly-trained soldiers armed with force pikes, a type of melee weapon with a vibro-edged head.

THE IMPERIAL MACHINE

The Death Star isn't the only means that the Empire uses to enforce its iron will.

THE IMPERIAL MACHINE

DROIDS, SHIPS, AND TECHNOLOGY

C2-B5

A black-plated astromech droid, C2-B5 patrols the Scarif Citadel, performing maintenance tasks. The subject of frequent memory wipes, C2-B5 has no distinctive personality.

ZETA-CLASS SHUTTLE

A cargo shuttle built under the cooperation of the Telegorn Corporation and the Sienar Fleet systems, the Zeta class offers assorted transportation options. 2 wing-mounted heavy laser cannons and 3 hull-mounted laser cannons offer useful defensive support.

AT–ACT

Designed as a cargo transport and not a combat vehicle like the AT-AT, the AT-ACT can still defend itself from attackers thanks to the two heavy cannons mounted on either side of its "head."

KX SERIES
A highly-mobile, highly-adaptable series of droid.

AT-ST

The All Terrain Scout Transport is a light walker, which serves as a reconnaissance vehicle. The two chin-mounted guns have a range of 2km.

THE IMPERIAL MACHINE

DROIDS, SHIPS, AND TECHNOLOGY

TIE STRIKER
A streamlined starfighter, the experimental TIE Striker is designed specifically for atmospheric patrols over Imperial installations.

TIE FIGHTER
With its distinctive "scream" and instantly recognizable silhouette the Imperial TIE fighter is the Empire's most common symbol of oppression.

MSE-6 DROID
A familiar sight at any Imperial installation, the MSE-6 "mouse" droids are fast-moving workers that relay coded messages and transport small items.

TX-225 "OCCUPIER"
Able to carry crucial supplies of kiber crystals, this maneuverable tank boasts immense firepower, as well as resilient armor.

THE
DEATH
STAR

Constructing a
technological terror...

THE DEATH STAR
CONSTRUCTING A TECHNOLOGICAL TERROR

> "We need to capture the Death Star plans if there is any hope of destroying it."
>
> *Jyn Erso*

The Empire rules by fear and intimidation, whether it's the shock attack of a unit of stormtroopers, the relentless march of a squadron of Imperial walkers, or the looming threat of a Star Destroyer in orbit above a planet. Yet while those measures can prove devastating on individual worlds, nothing before or since has spread interstellar terror like the Death Star.

A mobile battle station with hyperdrive capabilities, the Death Star is the size of a small moon and has the power to destroy an entire planet with a single shot of its superlaser, regardless of planetary defenses. It also houses many squadrons of TIE fighters, and hundreds of thousands of Imperial military personnel.

The earliest plans for the Death Star were conceived by the weaponsmiths of Geonosis at the outset of the Clone Wars. Then referred to simply as "the ultimate weapon," the design was commissioned by the Sith Lord Darth Tyranus, who was known publicly as Count Dooku. Acting on behalf of his master, Darth Sidious, Dooku headed the Confederacy of Independent Systems, a puppet movement of separatists in conflict with the Republic, set up to secretly advance the cause of the Sith. In his public capacity as Supreme Chancellor Palpatine, Sidious was in charge of the Republic, meaning that he was actually pulling the strings of both sides from behind the scenes.

When Geonosis was invaded by the Republic's army of clone troopers (on a mission to rescue a team of Jedi Knights), Geonosian leader Poggle the Lesser turned over the plans for the Death Star to Dooku, little suspecting that he was secretly a Sith Lord.

Construction of the Ultimate Weapon began in orbit of Geonosis soon after, and kyber crystals were gathered from far and wide to power its devastating superlaser. Work on the battlestation was well underway by the end of the Clone Wars, when Sidious disposed of his Confederacy underlings, including Dooku, and took on a new apprentice, Darth Vader, formerly the Jedi Knight Anakin Skywalker.

As Palpatine, Sidious declared himself Emperor of a new Galactic Empire, and took over the development of the Ultimate Weapon. He appointed Admiral Wilhuff Tarkin to supervise construction—with the help of Rear Admiral Tiaan Jerjerrod—and assigned Director Orson Krennic to oversee security for the project. Everything about the Death Star was kept top secret, with access to Geonosis severely restricted and the construction site guarded by several Star Destroyers and other Imperial ships.

The sheer scale of the project required a great deal of labor, much of it forced. Enslaved Wookiees and other species carried out much of the legwork, while Krennic enlisted scientists such as his old friend Galen Erso to apply their genius intellects to the technical challenges. Having been misled by Krennic, when Erso discovered what he was really working on, he fled Coruscant with his family, but was eventually captured.

Erso's decision to flee was not the only incident to dog the smooth development of the Death Star. Sentinel Base, a support facility on a nearby moon, was attacked by a group of former Republic Intelligence operatives ▶

THE DEATH STAR
CONSTRUCTING A TECHNOLOGICAL TERROR

1 /

2 /

3 /

THE DEATH STAR
CONSTRUCTING A TECHNOLOGICAL TERROR

4 /

acting under the orders of the Empire's own Vice Admiral Rancit. The admiral intended to betray his underlings to secure a promotion from the Emperor, but his plot was uncovered and he and his co-conspirators were captured, tortured, and eventually killed. In another incident, a small band of rebels based on the planet Lothal managed to destroy a single, massive kyber crystal that was en route to the Death Star to power its superlaser, delaying its completion.

After these setbacks, the Emperor decided to move the almost-completed Death Star from Geonosis to the planet Scarif. He also went so far as to have the entire population of Geonosis wiped out in order to ensure the continued confidentiality of the project.

This monstrous act did not succeed in keeping the Death Star entirely secret, however, and when the battlestation was finally complete, Galen Erso managed to send a coded transmission to the Alliance to Restore the Republic, telling them that a major Imperial weapons test was soon to take place. This led to the Alliance moving against the Empire with a plan to steal the schematics for the mysterious weapon, in the desperate hope they might discover some weakness…

THE DEATH STAR

CONSTRUCTING A TECHNOLOGICAL TERROR

Previous spread:
1 / The Death Star orbits Jedha.

2 / The ominous outline of the Death Star over Scarif.

3 / The rebels survey their target.

This spread:
4 / The superlaser dish is fitted to the battle station.

5 / Death Squad commanders on board.

ROGUE ONE CONCEPT ART
The illustrations that helped create the movie.

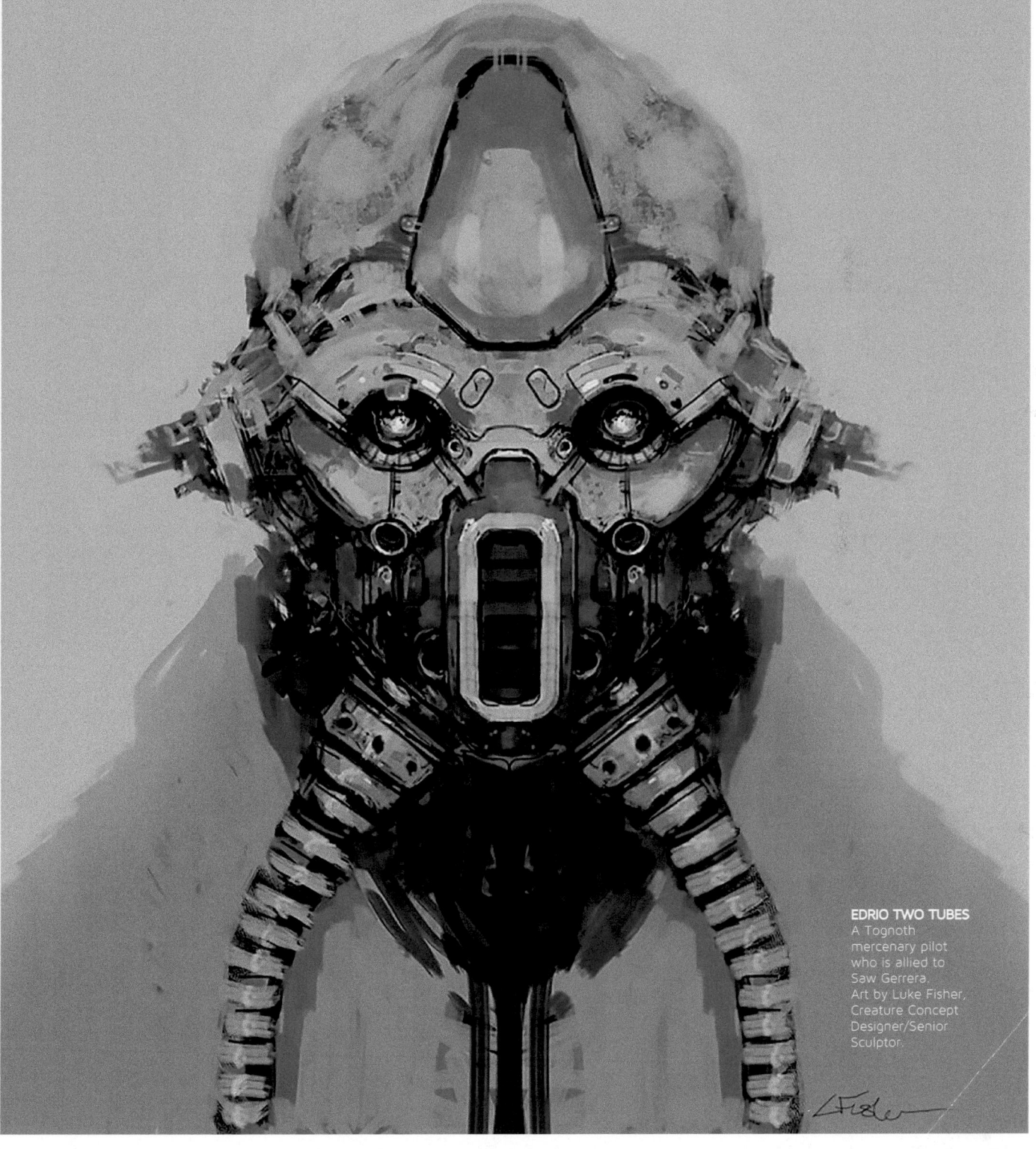

EDRIO TWO TUBES
A Tognoth mercenary pilot who is allied to Saw Gerrera. Art by Luke Fisher, Creature Concept Designer/Senior Sculptor.

**Opposite page:
SAW GERRERA**
The militia leader who operates from the catacombs on the mysterious world of Jedha. Art by Glyn Dillon, Co-Costume Designer.

ORSON KRENNIC
The director of the program to create the Imperial Death Star. Art by Glyn Dillon, Co-Costume Designer.

Opposite Page: CHIRRUT ÎMWE AND BAZE MALBUS
Two warriors from Jedha who prove crucial in the mission against the Empire.
Art by Glyn Dillon, Co-Costume Designer.

K-2SO
Imperial droid turned valuable asset in the fight to steal the Death Star plans.
Art by Luke Fisher, Creature Concept Designer/Senior Sculptor.

ROGUE ONE: A STAR WARS STORY | 95

JEDHA
The ancient Holy City of Jedha. Art by Matt Allsopp, Lead Concept Artist.

A TANK TROOPER Patroling the streets of Jedha, the tank troopers maintain control against insurgent forces. Art by Glyn Dillon, Co-Costume Designer.